Disney PRINCESS

Pretty Bedroom

Things to Make and Do

PaRragon

Bath • New York • Singapore • Hong Kong • Cologne • Delhi
Melbourne • Amsterdam • Johannesburg • Auckland • Shenzhen

First published by Parragon in 2011

Parragon
Queen Street House
4 Queen Street
Bath BA1 1HE, UK

ISBN 978-1-4454-2163-6
Printed in China.

Contents

Tips for Success

Remember, everything in this book should be made with the supervision and help of a grown up! A step labelled with "Kids" means that a child can do this step on their own. Some items will need to purchased from a supermarket or a craft/hobby store.

1 Prepare your space

Cover your workspace with newspaper or a plastic or paper tablecloth. Make sure you are wearing clothes (including shoes!) that you don't mind becoming spattered with food, paint or glue. But relax! You'll never completely avoid mess; in fact, it's part of the fun!

2 Wash your hands

Wash your hands before starting a new project, and clean up as you go along. Clean hands make for clean crafts! Remember to wash your hands afterwards too, using soap and warm water to get off any of the remaining materials.

3 Follow steps carefully

Follow each step carefully, and in the sequence in which it appears. We've tested all the projects; we know they work, and we want them to work for you, too.

4 Measure precisely

If a project gives you measurements, use your ruler, measuring scales, or measuring spoons to make sure you measure as accurately as you can. Sometimes, the success of the project may depend on it.

5 Be patient

You may need to wait while something bakes or leave paint, glue or clay to dry, sometimes for a few hours or even overnight. Be patient! Plan another activity while you wait, but it's important not to rush something as it may affect the outcome!

6 Clean up

When you've finished your project, clean up any mess. Store all the materials together so that they are ready for the next time you want to make and do. If you are making something with someone else then ensure it is a team effort!

Beautiful Bird Bath

Jasmine loves to watch birds from her bedroom window. Entice pretty birds into your garden with this bird bath and listen to them sing!

You will need

- A plain terracotta pot and base
- Strong glue
- Paint & brushes
- A cork
- A pen or cotton bud
- Leaves

Kids 1

Turn the pot upside down. Dip the cork (or thumb print) into white paint and print flower petals onto the pot. Print coloured dots around the edge.

Kids 2

Brush green paint onto the (real) leaves. Press onto the pot to print leaf shapes.

3

Use a cotton bud to print pink or yellow dots into the middle of the petals. Add a stripe to the middle of the leaves. Leave to dry.

Place the saucer on top of the pot and fill the saucer with water.

Heart Pillow Case

Aurora's royal bed spreads are covered in beautiful hearts. Sleep like a princess with this pillow case!

1

Push a piece of card inside the pillowcase. Tape the edges to a covered work surface. Place a cut-out card heart in the middle of the pillow case to use as a guide for printing.

You will need

- A plain white pillowcase
- Heart shape cut from card
- A pencil
- A cork
- A felt pen
- Fabric paint
- Saucer

Kids 2

Pour a small amount of fabric paint into a saucer. Dip a cork into the paint. Use it to print dots around the card heart shape. Dip the cork back into the paint after every two or three dots.

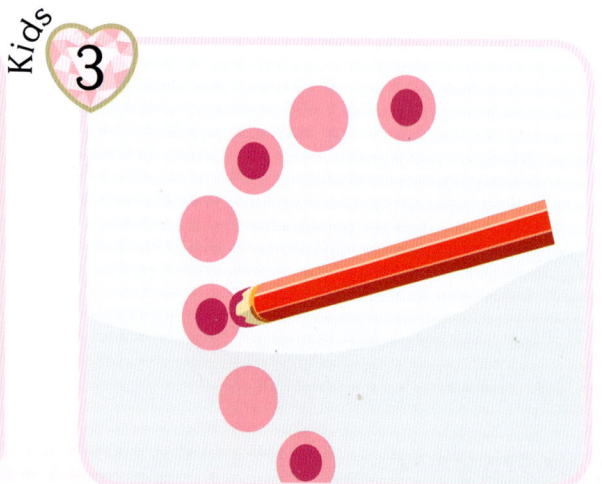

Kids 3

Use the end of a pen dipped into another colour to print smaller dots inside the bigger dots.

4

Take away the card heart and print another smaller heart shape using different colours inside the bigger heart. Leave to dry thoroughly, then put a pillow inside the case. Sweet dreams.

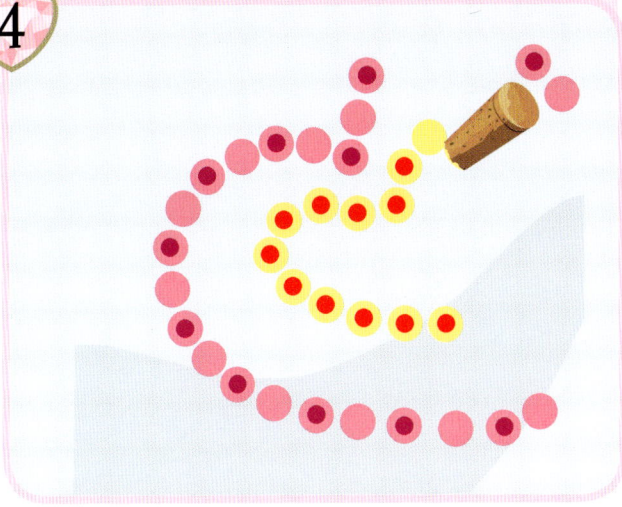

Aurora's tip:
Hearts are only one shape you can try. Why not come up with a starry print design?

Rose Magazine Holder

As you know, Belle loves to read. To keep your books or magazines tidy in your room, make this rose inspired holder!

1

Paint the box all over in a cream colour. Leave to dry.

You will need

- A plain file box – or a grocery box cut to the same shape
- Scissors
- Glue
- Paints
- Brushes
- Tissue paper
- A piece of rectangular sponge

2

Tear some strips of tissue paper 20 x 4 inches (50 x 10cm). Twist the strips round into a spiral for the roses then brush glue onto the end so the tissue paper doesn't unwind. Twist some green tissue strips for the stems.

3

Use a piece of rectangular sponge to print a brick pattern onto the box. Leave to dry.

4

Lay the box flat on your worksurface, then stick the stems and flowers onto the sides. (this is easier than doing it standing up). Add some cut out tissue paper leaves.

11

Fabulous Florals

Snow White loves exploring the woods and discovering sweet smelling flowers. When she needs somewhere to display her flowers she makes this wonderful vase!

You will need

- A clear vase
- String
- Pebbles
- Marbles
- Beads
- Sparkly gems

Kids 1

Carefully place some rocks inside the vase to cover the bottom.

2

Tie the flowers together with a piece of string and place them into the vase. Push the stems between the rocks so they stand up.

Kids 3

Add some more rocks, marbles and gems around the flowers until the vase is nearly full.

4

Use a jug or watering can to fill the vase with water. It will be very heavy so ask someone to lift it for you. It will look good near a window where the light can shine through.

Snow White's tip:
You can use plastic flowers for a permanent allergy free display!

Precious Display Case

Ariel has many trinkets and treasures from the ocean. To present them and keep them safe she has made her own display case. Make your own, it's easy and looks very special!

1

Glue the boxes together. Trim the edges first if they need to be made smaller. Leave to dry.

You will need

- Some small boxes
- Glue
- Paints
- Brush
- Glitter

2

Paint inside the boxes. Make sure your brush reaches into the corners.

3

Paint the outside using a different colour. Leave to dry.

Tip the boxes over on one side and brush with glue and sprinkle with glitter. Do the same on the other side and on the top.

Ariel's tip:
Put your most treasured item at the top of your case, and show it off properly!

Magical Lamp Holder

This magical holder is perfect for your bedside. Jasmine keeps her jewellery inside hers. What will you keep inside yours? Will a genie appear?

You will need

- Air drying clay
- Plastic knife
- Rolling pin
- Talcum powder
- A small bowl
- Some water in a bowl
- Pencil
- Paint
- Brush
- Gemstones

1

Roll out some clay to about ½ inch (15mm) thick and cut a circle shape 6 inches (15cm) diameter. Shake some talcum powder inside a small bowl then press the clay into the bowl.

2

Carefully release the clay, using a plastic knife if you need to (the talcum powder should help make it easier). Turn the clay shape over to flatten the top.

3

Roll a coil of clay for the handle. Smooth it down on one side of the lamp. Cut a triangular spout from rolled out clay and press a coil to the base. Use a pencil to make dot patterns and a hole in the spout.

4

Turn the lamp over and leave it to dry out. Support the spout with some rolled up paper whilst it is drying.

5

Paint and glue gems around the sides and leave to dry. Add your treasures!

Jasmine's tip:
Your lamp doesn't have to be gold. Paint it in any colour you like!

Musical Tin

Tiana lives in the Bayou, a place full of music! Make this musical themed tin and add some cheer to your room!

1

Cut out three small ovals (approx. ¾ inch (2cm) diameter) and thin strips from craft foam. Stick them onto some thick card into music note shapes. Do this in reverse so the printed design will look correct.

You will need

- A biscuit or cake tin with a lid
- A strip of paper long enough to wrap around a tin
- A paper circle to fit the lid
- Tape
- Craft foam
- Scissors
- Card
- Glue
- Paint
- Brush
- Glitter glue

2

Tape thin strips of folded card onto the top of the printing blocks so they are easy to hold. Tape the strip of paper (for the tin) to your work space.

3

Brush paint over the music notes then press down firmly onto the paper. Re-paint the block after making each print. Add spirals with glitter glue. Leave to dry. Print a design onto a paper circle in the same way for the lid.

4

Wrap the strip around the tin and tape the ends together. Glue the circle to the lid. Put some tasty treats inside. Or use as room storage to keep stationary or jewellery inside.

Tiana's tip:
Now you have a printing block you can use again. Try using it on something else!

Pretty Scented Bags

This pretty scented bag is filled with sweet smells! If you place it in your drawer, it will keep your clothes smelling sweet like flowers.

You will need

- Tray
- Lavender flowers
- Rose petals
- Thin fabric 4 x 12 inches (10 x 30cm)
- Fabric glue
- Rubber band
- Coloured ribbon
- Scissors
- Coloured felt or fabric scraps
- Beads or sequins (optional)

Kids 1

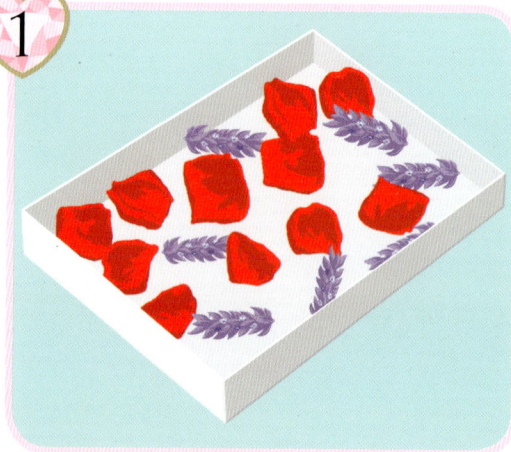

Spread out the lavender flowers and rose petals on a tray and allow them to dry for a couple of weeks.

Kids 2

Glue along the long sides of the fabric. Fold in half to make a bag. Press the edges together. Let dry.

Kids 3

Place some of the dried flowers inside the bag and gather the top together with a rubber band, then tie the ribbon on top.

4

Cut out small shapes from fabric or felt and glue them onto the bag. Glue on beads or sequins for extra decoration.

Cinderella's tip:
Place these bags in your clothes drawer or under your pillow!

Bird Feeder

Snow White loves this bird feeder because she loves to help her bird friends.

You will need

- Empty, rinsed-out juice carton with a nozzle
- Sandpaper
- Scissors
- Acrylic paints
- Paintbrush
- Bird seed
- Garden wire
- Mesh netting bag
- Varnish

1 Rub the outside of the carton with sandpaper until it's rough. Cut out a rectangular hole on the side facing away from the nozzle.

Kids 2 Paint the carton all over in one colour. This one is brown to look like tree bark.

Kids 3 After the paint is dry, add different shades and colours. This one has knots and vines, just like bark.

4

Add leaves or other decorations in a different colour. When you've finished painting, add a coat of varnish to help protect the feeder during cold and wet months.

5

Fill the mesh netting bag with birdseed, then push it through the rectangular hole in the feeder. Remove the nozzle, then pull the top of the bag through the spout. Next, thread wire through the top of the bag and twist the ends together. Hang the feeder up outside.

Snow White's tip:
Hang from a washing line if you don't have a tree in your garden!

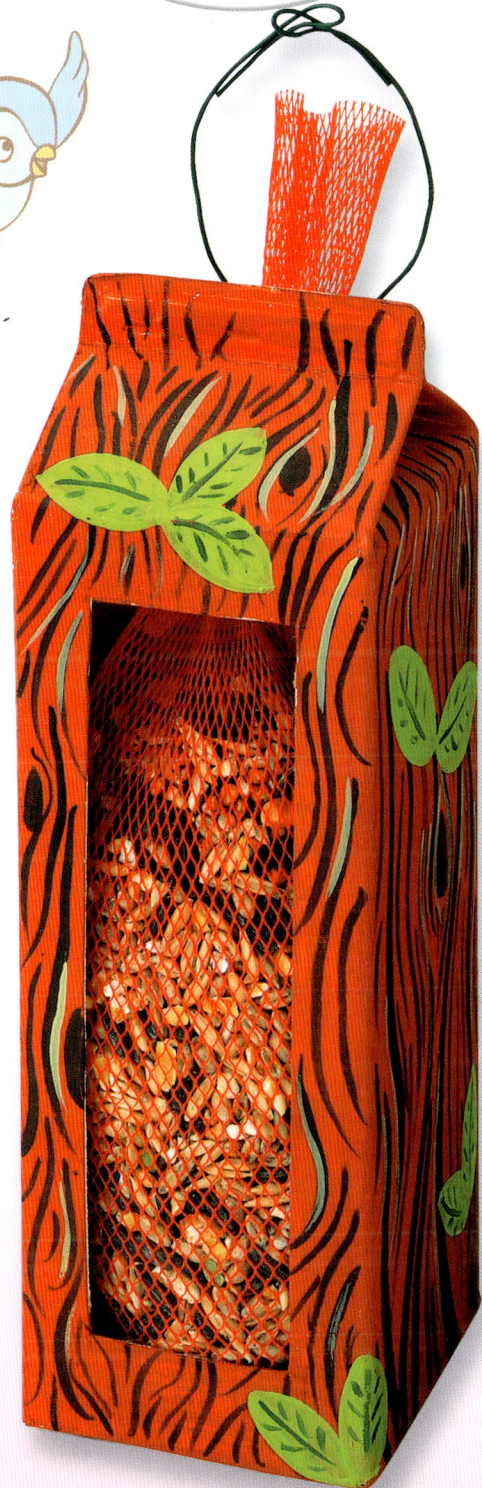

Candy Cushions

These comfy, candy-shaped cushions look good enough to eat, a bit like Tiana's beignets! Make a pile and turn your bedroom into a candy shop!

Kids

1

Glue the two pieces of fabric together, one on top of the other, along the longer edges. Glue the short edges together to make a tube. Put newspaper inside to stop the glued seam from sticking to the other side.

You will need

- For each cushion:
- 1 piece of gold-coloured fabric and 1 piece of coloured netting both 20 x 28 inches (30 x 70cm)
- Newspaper
- White glue and brush
- 2 strong rubber bands
- Cushion filling, such as polyester filling
- ½ yard (45cm) gold ribbon

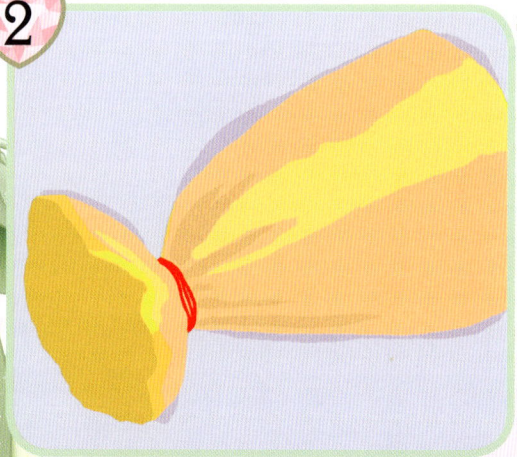

2

Once dry, gather up one end about 5 inches (13cm) from the edge and hold it in place with one of the rubber bands.

Kids

3

Start stuffing the cushion with the filling until it is filled to about 5 inches (13cm) from the top.

4

5

Close the end with the other rubber band. Fan out the ends of the cushion to make them look like candy wrappers.

Glue some gold ribbon over the rubber bands so they don't show.

Tiana's tip:
Recycle old cushions by picking apart the seams and reusing the filling for your groovy new cushions.

Shimmer & Shine Frame

Make a perfect picture frame from foil and old cardboard. Nobody will ever guess you've been recycling!

You will need

- Thick cardboard 5 x 5 inches (12 x 12cm)
- Thin cardboard 6 x 6 inches (15 x 15cm)
- Ruler
- Scissors
- Tin foil 8 x 8 inches (20 x 20cm)
- White glue and brush
- Old ballpoint pen

1

Measure and cut out a 2 x 2 inch (5 x 5cm) square hole from the middle of the thick cardboard.

2

Glue the card to the non-shiny side of the foil. Make a hole in the foil and make cuts toward each corner. Fold the triangles you've made onto the back of the frame and glue them down.

3

Put a line of glue round the cardboard and glue the four foil edges to it.

To make a stand, cut out a triangle of cardboard and tape it to the square of thin card as shown. Then glue the two squares of card together around three sides, leaving a slot at the top.

Slide a photo into the slot in the frame. Using the empty ballpoint pen, mark your design on the frame. Don't press too hard or you may tear the foil.

Ariel's tip:
You could even cut out a heart-shaped frame and decorate it with heart shapes cut from foil candy wrappers.

Starry Pen Tube

Make a tube to hold pens, pencils, or crayons for yourself or give it as a gift. This one is designed like the night sky with stars and comets.

1

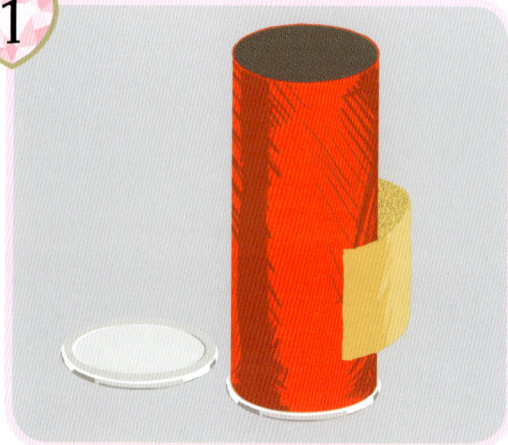

Lightly rub the tube all over with sandpaper. This will help the paint stick better to the tube.

You will need

- Cardboard tube with lid
- Fine sandpaper
- Black acrylic paint
- Paintbrush
- White glue and brush
- Glitter: gold, silver
- Scrap paper
- Sequins and star stickers

Kids 2

Cover the tube in black acrylic paint. Let dry, then apply another coat. Let the tube dry thoroughly.

Kids 3

Brush some glue onto the tube then sprinkle the glitter over the top. Shake off the excess glitter onto a piece of scrap paper.

4

Add the star stickers. Glue a row of sequins around the top and bottom of the tube, or anywhere to make your pen tube shimmer.

Belle's tip:
Stars shine brightly at night. This would make a wonderful gift for someone who you think is a super star!

Colourful Flower Pot

Flowers come in all shapes and sizes, and some of them smell so pretty. Make a special pot to keep your favourite bunch of flowers in. Place it in your window and watch your flowers grow!

You will need

- Flower-patterned gift wrap or pictures of flowers from magazines
- White glue and brush
- Plastic flowerpot

1

Cut out the prettiest flower shapes from the gift wrap or magazines.

2

Brush glue around the outside of the plastic flowerpot.

3

Glue the cut-out flowers to the flowerpot. Overlap them to make a pretty pattern.

Brush a thin layer of glue over the cut-outs to make the pot waterproof.

Aurora's tip:

You can decorate some pots with pictures of different leaves, or butterflies, or anything else you like.

Bright Room Tidy

Wastepaper baskets can be beautiful. Cover yours in some brightly coloured gift wrap. There's no need to hide your basket anymore!

You will need

- Round cardboard waste basket
- Roll of gift wrap
- Scissors
- White glue diluted with equal amount of water
- Paintbrush

1

Choose gift wrap that you like. Cut a piece a bit larger than the container. Wrap the paper around the container and glue it in place.

2

Make small snips in the top and bottom edges, fold them over and glue them down.

Cinderella's tip:
Ask a grown up about recycling the paper once you've filled your basket.

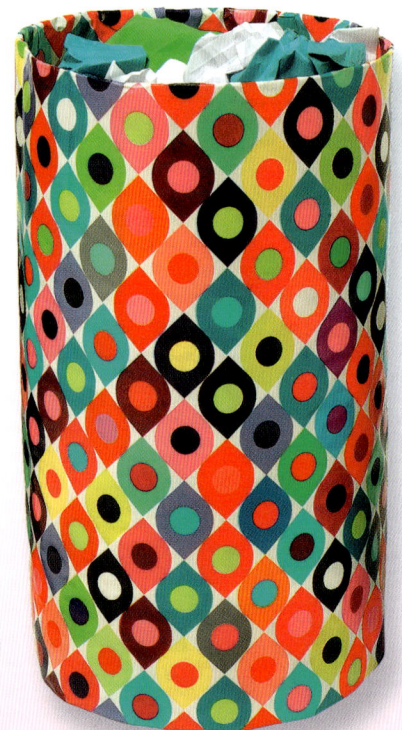